The Serenity Prayer
From Four Perspectives

Eva Dimel

Dr. Arvil Jones

The Serenity Prayer
From Four Perspectives

ISBN 978-1-940609-89-8 Soft cover

This book was printed in the United States of America.
To order additional copies of this book contact:
You Can Contact Dr Arvil Jones At... cjones156@cinci.rr.com or
By Calling 1-513-907-7751
Eva Dimel At.... EDime9775@sbcglobal.net or
By Calling 1-614-875-9263

Published by
FWB Publications
Columbus, Ohio

FWB

Table of Contents

Introduction

Again it is with grateful hearts that Eva Dimel and I are able to share another one of our joint efforts with all of you, our dear friends. If any of you have known someone who has, or is now going through any form of addiction, you know the trauma and heartache that are often connected with it, not only for the person who is addicted, but for the parents, and oftentimes the children of the addict. And in many cases, close friends are also affected. Both Eva and I have known our share of the heartache and sorrow associated with drug and alcohol addiction. But we also know there is help.

It could be argued from now till the end of time whether or not there is a cure for alcohol and drug addiction. There are some who contend that accepting the Lord Jesus Christ as personal Savior is the instantaneous and permanent *"cure-all"* for every addiction known to man, while others believe that once an addiction is medically and scientifically confirmed, the addict remains an addict for life, and there is no instantaneous and permanent cure. Somewhere between these two opposing views lies the truth.

While the salvation which can only be found in Jesus Christ is definitely the one and only cure for man's greatest problem – the problem of sin in the soul, that salvation does not guarantee instantaneous deliverance from any addiction, or the long-term effects and consequences of the addiction. And while it is entirely possible for God to instantaneously deliver anyone from any kind or degree of addiction, medical and scientific research and records, along with the testimonies of countless addicts themselves, show that the greatest number of addicts require ongoing medical treatments and qualified counseling for the rest of their lives. The sad truth, then, is that neither God nor science is the instantaneous or permanent "cure-all" for addiction. But, thankfully, there are thousands of cases in which God, science, and the addict come together, and cooperate with one another, producing a lasting and effectual "recovering" from addiction. And that is the happy medium between the two opposing views – the fact that an addict does not have to give up all hope, for there is hope – hope for a healthy, happy, and productive life. The only requirement of the addict is that he or she seek the help that brings the hope.

The Serenity Prayer
From Four Perspectives

Dedication

We would like to dedicate this booklet to God our Father, for without Him this book would not have been possible to write. He holds everything we need in life in His heart, His hands, and His Love for us. He has shown us time and again that all things are possible with Him, and that includes whatever it is whoever is reading this may be going through right now. Addiction is not an easy road to travel for anyone involved, including the ones who love the addict and the addict themselves. But it is a road which you don't have to travel alone, and it is not a road to nowhere, it is not a road with no end. God is and always will be there by your side to help you in every way, and with every step. And having had firsthand experience with addicts, and seeing them on the road to recovery, we thank God for His tender mercies.

We also dedicate this little booklet to every addict in the world, whether you have recently become addicted, or are a recovering addict. We also dedicate this booklet to the parents, children, and friends of the addict. And finally, we dedicate this booklet to all the doctors, nurses, counselors, and ministers who have given of their time and talents in an effort to save the life of a fellow human being from destruction.

Eva Dimel,
Dr. Arvil Jones

The Serenity Prayer -
From Four Perspectives

The Serenity Prayer
From Four Perspectives

Chapter One

The Addict

God grant me the serenity to accept the things I cannot change. Grant me the peace that passes all understanding, so that I may understand there are so many things, situations, and circumstances in life, and so many questions, even about myself, to which I am incapable of finding the answers – things that are simply too high for me. There are times when I really think I do understand - only to discover again that I am wrong, and that my way is not your way. And the more I try my way the more I fail, and so I give up, and continue doing the things that are destroying not only my life but the lives of those I love also. And here I am again, asking you Lord to please grant me that serenity, because I cannot find it by myself.

Lord, I am not making excuses, and I am not blaming anyone but myself for the situation I have created, and for the consequences I know I must face as a result of my choices. Looking back on how this horrible addiction began, I now realize that it happened, not because I was incapable of resisting the temptation, but because I was unwilling to resist it. I simply made a conscious choice, knowing there might be harmful consequences, but never guessing how horrible things would become, not only for myself, but also for those I love. At the moment I took the first drink, and injected the first dose, I wasn't thinking of anyone but myself, and that ecstatic feeling of euphoria I was promised. And Lord, even though I had seen many others who had fallen victim to the same addictions, I gave in, and succumbed to the temptation.

I've tried so many times to change things, including myself, thinking I could make everything better, but so far nothing I've done has worked, and I realize, without you, I don't know what I'm doing. I have let so many people down with my unending promises to change things, and my countless failures to see any change have made me see the truth – the sad truth that I really didn't want to change. I had nearly convinced myself that nothing really needed to be changed, and that I am fine the way I am. Lord, the choices that I have made, and the consequences of those choices, have brought me to where I am – here, before you, in earnest prayer, knowing that who I am, and what I am, are not who I want to be. I acknowledge my need of your help Lord, for with you all things are possible. I have failed, but with your help I can succeed. And Lord, even as I ask for this sweet serenity, I'm beginning to understand that it is not you who needs my help, but it's me who needs your help. And so let this journey begin, as I watch you make the changes that really need to be made.

Lord grant me the courage to change the things I can, and one of those things is my own attitude. Although I cannot change the consequences of my choices, and although I may fear those consequences, give me the courage to face them like a man, whatever they may be. Grant me the courage to change my attitude toward others. Help me to see the pain and the tears of my family as a message and a reminder that my choices have hurt them, perhaps even more than I've hurt myself. My attitude toward them has been that their feelings don't matter, and I feel as if they are simply overreacting. My attitude has been that what I am doing is not that bad, even though it's all about me, and the things I want. I can change that attitude Lord, but I need the courage that only comes from you in order to do it. God grant me the courage to change my attitude toward my children. Lord, you know I love them, but I have not put them and their needs before my own, and in neglecting to put their needs before my own, I have demonstrated that I love myself more than I love them. I have done whatever I needed to do in order to get what I want while forgetting about them and their needs. I can change that attitude Lord, but I need the courage that only comes from you in order to do it.

Lord, grant me the courage to change my attitude toward my duties as a father and husband. I have gone from job to job, losing each one in an attempt to gratify my need. And in gratifying my need, I have neglected to pay the bills that must be paid. Satisfying my need has nearly destroyed everything around me, including my life. Lord, deep down inside I really want to be happy, and I want to be the person you created me to be. But if I am worth helping Lord, I need courage that only comes from you in order to leave this old person behind, and accept the person you make of me. I hear you whisper to my heart - *"You are my child whom I love so much. Your value to me and the ones who truly love you could never be measured."* Thank you Lord, I needed to hear that.

And Lord, while I'm here on my knees, I find myself searching for the proper words with which to say what I want to say. I realize that I, within myself, do not have the power to change the life of anyone else. And Lord, even though I made that conscious choice to take my first drink of alcohol, and to inject that first hit into my veins, I still can see the face of the one who offered it to me. And

Lord, I know I'm not the only one – I am only one among many thousands who made the wrong choice. But Lord, if somehow through your infinite wisdom and mercy you can use me and my addiction to show someone else how horrible it is to be totally helpless, and totally dependent upon a drug or a drink in order to survive another day, then I am willing to pay whatever price is necessary if it will prevent them from making that same bad choice.

Lord grant me the wisdom to know the difference between the things I cannot change, and the things I can, for I have often failed to discern between the two. Lord, you see my awful plight – I have neither the serenity to accept the things I cannot change, the courage to change the things I can, nor the wisdom to know the difference. And the absence of that serenity, courage, and wisdom has plunged me into my present condition. If I were wise I would not be making the choices I've been making, knowing beforehand the destruction that was certain to follow. Everything is falling apart, I'm losing the ones that I love, and no one trusts me anymore. Most of my friends and family don't even want to be around me anymore, because they see the sad results of the unwise choices I have made. My lack of wisdom tends to make me feel as if they are the ones with a problem instead of me. I've told myself, and them, that they are the ones who need to change, and accept me for who and what I am. Even when they have tried to help me so many times, I didn't have the wisdom to see what they were trying to do for me. My failure, my neglect, my refusal to see that others only wanted to help me - all of these, prove my lack of wisdom. My lack of wisdom, courage and serenity have caused me to become mean and hateful, even to the point that I was not content with being miserable by myself, but wanted to make everyone else's life miserable also.

And now Lord, I am alone, homeless, with nowhere to go. My body and spirit seem to be falling apart, piece by piece. A few times I have almost died, chasing after the one thing I have loved, that one thing that has been killing me slowly, a little bit more every day. A few times I've wanted to die rather than go on living this way, and even thought of what would be the quickest and least painful way of ending it all. So Lord, here is what you have to work with – a broken and helpless person at his wits end, crying for help. And Lord, if you can be so gracious as to grant me the serenity, courage and wisdom I so desperately need, would it be asking too much if I also ask for the patience to wait for them?

───────·III·───────

Dear Lord, I'm a young lady, I'm eighteen, I'm an addict, and now I've discovered I'm going to be a mother. Lord, someone told me that you are a loving and patient heavenly Father who listens to and answers prayer. Another friend of mine, a young man who is also an addict and a father, told me about a place where he goes regularly for counseling. He said the whole group prays something called The Serenity Prayer, in which they ask you for the serenity to accept the things they cannot change, the courage to change the things they can, and the wisdom to know the difference. Well, Lord, as you know, I've developed a lot of habits in my young life, but praying was not one of them, so if I make a lot of blunders here, I hope you'll understand. Those three things are certainly things I need right now. I guess you could say I've come to the point of desperation. I have nowhere to go, and I have no one to turn to. I am afraid and ashamed to go home to my family now, because I don't know how either of my parents will take the news that their addicted daughter is also going to be an unwed mother.

Lord, I've really messed up, and I've run out of excuses for my behavior, and now I realize that, as bad as my situation is with my addiction, now there is another life that is also affected. The doctors tell me my baby will be born addicted. And as if that is not horrible enough, the folks from Children's Services are telling me that I only have two choices – abort the baby, or give her up for adoption. Lord, I'm not a very religious person, but I do believe in the sanctity of life. I absolutely refuse to abort my baby, even though my boyfriend and some other folks are insisting that I do. So Lord, as far as needing the serenity to accept the things I cannot change, I cannot change the fact that

I am an addict, I cannot change the fact that I am going to be an unwed mother, and I cannot change the fact that my precious baby will be born an addict. And yes Lord, I'm finding all of those realities very hard to accept.

Lord, before I discovered I was pregnant, in all honesty, I have to admit I really didn't want to change. Along with some powerful persuasion from those who have supplied my addiction, I convinced myself it was my destiny to live and die as a hopeless addict, with no prospects for any kind of happiness, or a family of my own. But now that I am pregnant, I realize my life is not just about me now – it's about this precious child inside of me, and her future. I know there are some things I can, and must change for my baby's sake, but Lord I need the courage to do them. I have wallowed in my self-pity for too long, and that is something I can change. Lord, I need the courage to face those whom I have hurt so deeply, and to try to make amends in any way I can. I need the courage to face those who have coerced me into prolonging my addiction by supplying me

with the drugs and alcohol, and to tell them I
no longer want to be a helpless and hopeless
addict. I need the courage to face the truth
that my life has been an artificial life, an
artificial means of coping with realities.

And Lord, I have no idea how my
family is going to react when I tell them the
whole truth, but I know I must tell them. How
do I tell my dear mother that I sold my body
for the price of an injection? How do I tell my
Dad I slept in an alley with only a cardboard
box for shelter rather than face him, and tell
him the truth? And how do I go on living if my
baby is taken from me, and given to a total
stranger? And how am I supposed to live with
myself knowing I am the cause of her being
born with an addiction? Yes, Lord, I
understand there are things I cannot change,
and I pray for the serenity to accept them. I
know there are some things I can change, and
I pray for the courage to take the first step
toward changing them. But Lord, I also need
the wisdom to recognize the difference
between what I can and cannot change. I
have no doubt that when my family sees me,
they will look at me somewhat differently
than they did before I walked blindly into this

web of deceit from which I cannot untangle myself.

Lord, before I rise from my knees, I just want to add that, I am not blaming anyone else for my situation. I take full responsibility for the choices I've made, and I am willing to face whatever consequences may await me. But Lord, for the sake of this precious child in my womb, I beg for your mercy, your grace, and your patience with me as I begin this long journey toward recovery and, hopefully, some degree of reconciliation with my dear parents. Thank you for listening Lord.

Chapter Two

The Parent's Perspective

Lord, grant me the serenity, the calmness I need so desperately when it comes to dealing with the one I love – the person who is choosing all the wrong things in life, things that I know are not good, things that cause me to worry constantly, while I fear for their health, their safety, and their life. Sometimes I feel so weak and helpless dear God, and I know you are the only source of the peace and strength I need to get through each day.

Give me the peace and strength to accept the things I cannot change. I have tried everything I can possibly do to make everything better, and to help them to change. And when I fail to see any positive change in them, I get so angry at them, and I cry, and I feel so helpless. Some folks who know me often ask why I keep trying, and my answer is always the same -because I love them, and I don't want to lose them. I keep telling myself I can't do this, and it's not working, but when they mess up again I go running to their rescue, hoping and praying that this time I'll be able to make a difference somehow. But again I am disappointed – not only in their behavior, but in myself also. I feel that I must blame someone for the failures of my child, and who better to blame than myself. I often ask – Do they even care, or do they even realize I am trying to help them, or are they so addicted and dependent upon their habit that they don't realize what they're doing to me? Please help me Lord to realize, I have a life to live, a life which you gave me, and I cannot live my children's lives for them, even though I sometimes want to. Help me to accept the things I cannot change.

Lord, grant me the courage to change the things I can. Lord, if there is something – anything, in my own life that needs changing, please help me to see it, confront it, and do something about it. If there is something in my life that I can change which will be of any positive help to my child, I am ready and willing to change it immediately. I am so fearful of losing my child. It seems as if I have already lost the love, the respect, and the friendship we once enjoyed before the addiction began, and Lord, I want all that back. And as hard as it is to have lost their love, respect, and friendship, my greatest fear is that they may lose their life, and I will have lost them forever, and that is the one thing I am not prepared to face.

I have lost my joy, my happiness, and my peace. I am so wrapped up in what they are doing I don't realize how miserable I am until I am alone, and it hits me – I may lose my child to an addiction. And Lord, along with all the medical bills piling up, we are also faced with a lot of legal fees, paying fines, and for lawyers to keep our child out of jail. Many of our friends and neighbors, and a few judges, have told us that we are not doing our child any favors, but that we are actually enabling him by bailing him out every time he gets into trouble. If I keep doing this then there is not going to be enough money left for me to pay my bills. We have had to re-finance our home in order to make ends meet, and sometimes the ends don't meet at the end of the month. Please help me Lord; I need the courage to change the things I can in my own life.

And Lord, it doesn't happen often, but once in a while, during those moments when he is sober, and we can sit and talk for a while, he seems so different- as if there is absolutely nothing amiss. He can be so kind, courteous, and even loving. It is during those precious moments when I look into his eyes, and I think I can see a ray of hope there. He looks back at me with that beaming smile I used to love so much when he was a child, and he steals my heart again, making promises that he is never going to drink again, and never take another drug. And so I cave in again, and give him more money, believing his story, only to be devastated again when I get that phone call, telling me he is either in the hospital, or in jail. So I guess what I'm asking for Lord is the courage to say no to him – perhaps that is the change I need to make more than any other.

And grant me the wisdom to know the difference between what I cannot change and what I can change. Lord, I know your Holy Word teaches that wisdom which comes from above is pure, peaceable, and easy to be entreated. That is the wisdom I need – a God-given wisdom that will teach me the difference between helping my child and enabling him. Lord, you know that in my heart I want the addiction to end, and I'd be willing to do anything in my power to end it if I could. But I understand that this addiction, even though it has affected me and my whole family, is not all about me. I know some folks might not understand when I tell them I want you to have all the credit, the honor, and the glory in bringing this horrible nightmare to an end. Lord, give me the wisdom to let go of the things I cannot change, and turn them over to you. I'm casting my cares upon you Lord, because I know you care for me and my family. I guess I'll just have to confess Lord, I've been trying to do your job for you, and that's why I have failed so miserably.

After I have given, and given, and given, and there is nothing left to give, and I am forced to say no, my child turns on me, and tries to make me feel guilty, as if I have failed to be a good parent. I don't know which is worse –

the guilt I feel for having enabled my child to support the addiction, or the guilt, anger, and helplessness I feel when my child curses me to my face when I say no. As you can see, Lord, I am caught in a vicious cycle, a whirling vortex from which I cannot escape by my own wisdom. And Lord I pray that you will help my child to realize the same truth I have realized — that I am not the answer to the dilemma, but you are.

Chapter Three

A Child's Perspective.

Dear Lord, I'm just a child, and I know I don't understand a lot of things, but I've been told that you always hear the prayers of a child, so here I am Lord, and I sure hope you have some answers, 'cause I've got a lot of questions. Lord Jesus, some of my friends at school say that I shouldn't have to put up with all the stuff I have to see and hear at our house, but I told them I don't have much choice but to accept it, because I have nowhere else to go. Some of them tell me they are going through the same bad stuff at their house. I sure wish I could make my Daddy change Lord, 'cause he's really mean sometimes when he comes home. He hits my Mom really hard, and makes her cry a lot. Sometimes he takes her to another room and shuts the door, and I can hear my Mom screaming, begging my Dad not to hit her anymore.

Lord, I'm only ten, and I love my Mom and Dad, but he's so big and mean I can't make him stop hurting her. I got so mad at him once I tried to stop him, but he slapped me in my face, and shoved me down on the floor. Then he took off his belt, and whipped me hard. He told me if I ever tried to stop him again he would make me really sorry. Lord Jesus, it didn't used to be this way at my house when I was younger. I remember Dad and Mom taking me to Sunday school and church where I learned about you and all the good stuff you did for all of us. Lord, I know my Mom loves you, 'cause she's the one who taught me to pray to you like this. But I'm not so sure about my Dad. I don't know if he even loves me or Mom. Sometimes he acts like he don't love nobody but himself.

I guess you already know what's wrong at our house Lord, and I'm ashamed to say it to you, but Mom always told me to be honest when I pray, so Lord, my Daddy is on drugs and alcohol now, and he's just not the same

Daddy he was when I was little. He's changed so much that me and Mom sometimes think he's not the same man we once knew. He used to play catch with me, and take me to ball games and fishing, but now he says he can't afford to do that anymore 'cause he never has enough money. He sold my new bike to one of my friends for twenty dollars, and now I can't go riding with any of my friends, and some of them laugh at me 'cause I don't have a bike.

And Lord, a lot of the other kids at school make fun of me 'cause I have to wear second hand clothes, and some of them call me names, and make fun of my Dad and Mom, and call them white trash. My Dad has to go to jail a lot 'cause he does bad stuff when he takes his drugs, and the cops come and tell me and Mom he's in jail again. My Mom has to go and borrow money from somebody so we can have food to eat when Dad's in jail, 'cause sometimes he has to stay a long time. Lord, I hope You don't think I'm a big baby if I cry, but sometimes I can't help it, especially when my Mom tells me to take the last piece of bread and eat it, and she won't take any for herself.

Lord, you know I would change everything if I could, and make it all better for my Mom and Dad, but I just don't know what I can do to make it better. I guess I just have to live with it till I'm old enough to get a job and make money. Me and Mom get sick a lot Lord, and the last time we went the doctor, he said we were something called malnourished. I don't know what that means, but Lord, I sure am hungry, and I know Mom is too. But I guess my question for you is – am I supposed to accept my life the way it is, or should I try to change it and make it better somehow?

And Lord, if there is something I can change, I sure would like to know. Sometimes when my Dad is drinking or doing his drugs he tells me it's all my fault. He says if I hadn't come along when I did, him and Mom would get along better, and he wouldn't have to take drugs and do bad stuff. Some of my friends tell me I must be a really bad kid, 'cause Dads with good kids don't drink or get on drugs. Lord, if I'm a bad kid, I want to change and be better. But Lord I can't do it all by myself, 'cause I don't know where to start. Some of the other boys and girls at school tell me I'm poor and ugly, and that my Dad is ashamed of me, and doesn't love me, and that's why he started drinking and using drugs. Lord, what can I do to make Dad love me again, and not be ashamed of me? If it's my fault Lord, I'd rather just go away somewhere by myself so Mom and Dad can be happy again. One big boy at school told me I should kill myself and it would make my Dad happy. Lord, if that's what I have to do to make things better for Mom and Dad, I'll do it, but I hope you won't hold it against me.

I guess I've taken up too much of your time already Lord, but I know there are some things I can't change, and maybe there are some things I can, but in case I make a mistake and don't know the difference, will you show me somehow? I'm really counting on you here Lord, 'cause I can't go on like this much longer. I'm asking all of this in Jesus name, Amen. Oh, sorry Lord, I forgot to say goodnight. Tell Grandma and Grandpa Hi for me up there.

The Serenity Prayer
From Four Perspectives

Chapter Four

God's Perspective

My dear children, yes, I do always hear your prayers, and I never miss a word. At this very moment I am receiving many thousands of prayers just like yours from all over the world, and all for the same reason – someone has become addicted to drugs, alcohol, or both. You made the right choice in bringing your problem to me, and rest assured I will not ignore it. If only everyone would pray as earnestly and sincerely as you have prayed! That tender feeling you now feel in your heart is my Holy Spirit speaking to you. It's my way of saying that my own heart is touched by your grief and sadness – I feel the pain in your heart.

33

All of you may calmly rest assured that your prayers are being answered. In fact, I heard all of them even before you prayed, But because you have taken the time to come to me with an honest and sincere heart, seeking the answers you can't find anywhere else, I delight in giving you an answer of peace. To each of you – the child, the mother, and the addict himself, your answers have been so close to you for so long, as close as your Holy Bibles. My answer to every request you have made can be found written in the pages of my sacred Word.

You have asked for the serenity to accept the things you cannot change. Do you not remember when I was with my disciples out on the Sea of Galilee, when the great tempest frightened them nearly to death? Each of them was fearful of dying in that storm – a storm from which none of them could escape by their own skill. They all tried desperately to bring the ship to land, but the storm was too much for them, and so, when they finally realized they could not help themselves, or change the situation, they, as you have done, came to me. For their sakes, I demonstrated my Omnipotence and my love for them, rebuking the wind and the mighty waves. Do you not remember the great calm which followed? There, my children, in the pages of my Word, is where you will find the same serenity my first disciples sought, and found.

You have asked for the courage to change the things you can. My answer to each of you is the same as the first. The source of you serenity is the same source of your courage – my Holy Word. Do you not remember my servant David, who when only a lad, ran out to meet a giant more than three times his size? David had brothers who were older, bigger, and far more experienced than he in warfare, but none of them had the courage to go out and face Goliath. Even King Saul, who stood head and shoulders above every man in Israel, lacked the courage to face the fearful enemy. Saul compared Goliath to himself, and realized he was no match for him. David compared Goliath to my Son Jesus, and knew that He was more than a match. David was not born with the courage he needed to change the situation – he realized that all strength and courage comes only from the source of all strength and courage. With his God-given courage, David changed the course of history, and saved a nation from defeat. It is there, my children, in my Holy Word, that you will find the courage to change the things you can.

You have asked for the wisdom to know the difference between the things you cannot change and the things you can change. And again, I must send you to the only true source of wisdom – my Holy Word. Do you not remember the two mothers who each bore a child, and one of them lay upon her child one night, and the child died? That evil mother stole the child of the other mother, claiming him as her own. The real mother brought the matter to the wise King Solomon. Do you remember where King Solomon got all his wisdom? He prayed to me for wisdom and knowledge, and I answered him, making him the wisest king who ever lived. When the matter was brought before King Solomon, he took a very bold step, commanding the living child to be brought to him. Then he called for a sword, commanding that the child be cut in half, giving one half to each of the women.

Solomon, in his God-given wisdom, knowing the real mother would rather give the child to the other woman than see him divided in half, was exercising the kind of wisdom for which all of you have asked. Solomon could not change the evil heart of the mother who accidentally killed her own child, and claimed the other mother's son, but he could change the outcome of the situation, and he had the God-given wisdom to know the difference. My answer to each of you is the same - the serenity, the courage, and the wisdom you need are all right there, in that Book you have in your hand.

www.ingramcontent.com/pod-product-compliance
Lightning Source LLC
Chambersburg PA
CBHW060635030426
42337CB00018B/3380